Cooking
SOURDOUGH
in the
Backcountry

· *Tips, Tales & Recipes* ·

SCOTT E. POWER

ALPEN
BOOKS
PRESS

 Published by AlpenBooks Press, LLC
4602 Chennault Beach Road, B1
Mukilteo, WA 98275 USA
(425) 493-6380

Manufactured in the United States of America
Illustrations: Marge Mueller, Gray Mouse Graphics
Book and cover design: Marge Mueller, Gray Mouse Graphics
All text photos by the author

Library of Congress Cataloging-in-Publication Data

Power, Scott E., 1970-
  Cooking with sourdough in the backcountry : tips, tales and recipes / by Scott E. Power.
      p. cm.
  Includes bibliographical references and index.
  ISBN 0-9669795-7-5
  1. Cookery (Sourdough) 2. Bread. I. Title.

TX770.S66P685 2004
641.8'15—dc22
                                    2004013997

DEDICATION

This book is dedicated to the finest people I know:

*David Scott, my trip partner and friend. Dave is one of the
most sincere people I know, as well as one of the strongest
and most courageous. Without him,
I would have died several times over.*

*Dr. William W. Forgey (a. k. a. Doc), my dear friend and mentor who
made it all happen by giving his complete support to the
1991–1992 expedition.*

My family, who love me despite my crazy ways.

My friends, who love my crazy ways.

Channing Dungey, the love of my life.

The dining room table at Doc's cabin, set with sourdough goodies

Table of Contents

Foreword, William Forgey, M.D.   9
Introduction: Why Sourdough in the Backcountry?   11

PART ONE: BEGINNING   17

Chapter 1. Backcountry Baking Methods   19
Baking on a Campfire   20
The Reflector Oven   20
The Skillet Oven   21
The Dutch Oven   22
Baking on a Trail Stove   23
The Double-pan Oven   23
The Jell-O® Mold Oven   24
Baking on a Wood Stove   25
The Stovetop Camp Oven   26
The Dutch Oven   26

Chapter 2. Making Sourdough   27
Ingredients   27
Flour   28
Leaveners   29
Sweeteners   30
Fats   31
Egg Substitute   31

Containers for Sourdough   31

Special Instructions   32

Sourdough Starters and Batters   33

    Commercial Starter   33

    Homemade Starters   34

Primary Batter   34

PART TWO: RECIPES   35

Chapter 3. Appetizers   37

Boonie Bread Sticks   37

Pretzels   39

Salt Crackers   39

Scottish Scones   40

Wild Wheat Crackers   40

Chapter 4. Breads, Rolls and Biscuits   41

Trailblazin' Bannock   42

Biscuits   42

Bread Rolls   44

Cheddar Cheese Bread   44

Country Cornbread   45

English Muffins   45

No-knead Bread   46

No-knead Cornmeal-Raisin Bread   46

No-knead Colonial Bread   47

No-knead Peanut Butter Bread   47

Oatmeal Raisin Cakes   48

Raisin Muffins   48

Scott's Cabin Bread   49

French Bread   49

French Rolls   51

Chapter 5. Entrees   52

Country Fry Batter   53

Papa's Noobles   53

Pizza Crust   54

Dumplings   55

Chapter 6. Desserts   56

Bite-size Peanut Butter Cookies   58

Baker's Chocolate Cake   58

Dazzlin' Dave's French Quarter Beignets   59

Saturday Morning Cinnamon Rolls   60

Robin Hood Oatmeal Pudding   61

Mrs. Welburn's Oatmeal Raisin Cookies   62

Chapter 7. Pancakes and Waffles   63

Bacon Pancakes   65

Apple Pancakes   66

Chocolate Waffles   66

Cornmeal Pancakes   67

Cornmeal Waffles   67

Oat Pancakes   68

Rice Pancakes   68

Russian Pancakes   69

Sourdough Waffles   69

Traditional Sourdough Pancakes   70

Whole Wheat Pancakes   70

Whole Wheat Waffles   71

Top 10 Miscellaneous Uses of Sourdough   72

Epilogue   74

Appendices   75

A. Trail Stove Tips   76

B. Useful Common Weights and Measures   77

Bibliography   78

Index   78

Dave Scott and I built this cabin in the fall of 1991.

Foreword

BOOKS ON SOURDOUGH COOKING generally are steeped in the lore of the men and women who used sourdough. This book is no exception. But the story told by the young man who wrote it is exceptional. A year after finishing high school Scott Power traveled to the far north, 900 miles above the U.S. border, to a remote part of Manitoba, Canada. There he stayed with another young man his age for an entire year, cut off from all communication with the outside world, sheltered by a log cabin they built, and living on sourdough.

This is a book written from experience and from his passion for cooking one of the most delightful foods ever to be discovered. Scott's partner in this great adventure, Dave Scott, wrote a book about their experience titled *Paradise Creek*. In it he describes Scott's particular ability for cooking sourdough bread on their wood stove:

"I unloaded the .30-.30 and walked inside. The cabin was illuminated with the hissing light of a Coleman lantern and filled with the fragrance of freshly baked bread. I sliced off a hefty hunk of bread and stuffed it into my mouth . . . .

"Before I continue, I have to say that both Scott and I can bake delicious bread, however Scott is a master. When I was little both my mother and I would make a sandwich, yet for some reason hers always turned out better than mine and hers still do to this very day. It's all in the heart, and after tasting Scott's 'cabin' bread, one comes to the conclusion that he puts a great deal into each and every loaf he bakes."

And Scott puts a great deal of heart into this book.

It's surprising just how important eating, and therefore cooking, is during long wilderness trips. In fact, eating is frequently the single most important topic of conversation. Certain recipes bring with them a story of where they were found, be it on a box purchased in a mining town in Manitoba, given by

Mom on a 3 x 5 card, carefully written out by the wife of a local acquaintance, or hastily suggested by a bearded surveyor as he climbs back into his helicopter after an impromptu visit.

These stories, and others, form some of the fabric of this book; the recipes and ingredients form most of the rest. And then there is Scott's heart. That touch will make this the most unique cooking book in your kitchen.

William W. Forgey, M.D.
Crown Point, Indiana

Introduction

WHY SOURDOUGH IN THE BACKCOUNTRY?

IT WAS JANUARY 5, 1989, when I tried sourdough bread for the first time, while waiting out my six-hour layover at San Francisco airport. As I strolled through the airport I couldn't help but notice how proud San Francisco is of its sourdough heritage. It seemed every airport shop had a colorful display rack selling Genuine San Francisco Sourdough Bread. Little did I know how important sourdough bread would eventually become to me.

Throughout the Gold Rush of 1849, and even as far back as the ancient Egyptians, sourdough has played a part in maintaining a healthy and enjoyable diet. For me, it took living in a remote wilderness log cabin near the Arctic Circle to learn how versatile sourdough is, and how valuable it really is to one's backcountry menu.

Few people know the sensation of being left alone in an isolated wilderness, to fend for themselves without the help of "civilization." Living alone in a remote wild terrain is not something many people care about doing these days. However, for Dave Scott and me, two 20-year-olds from northwest Indiana, it was our dream to see what lessons Mother Nature would teach us when given the chance. So the dream became a goal: plan a trip to a remote cabin in northern Canada and live there for one year, experiencing all four seasons.

The cabin we sought use of was built in 1975 by Dr. William W. Forgey, the "Father of Wilderness Medicine" and author of *Wilderness Medicine*. Nestled off the shores of Hudson's Bay in the black spruce pines of northern Manitoba, Canada, "Doc" Forgey's cabin was perfect for our dream camping trip. Upon hearing our request, Doc didn't hesitate to grant us permission to use his cabin. From that moment on he played a key role in planning the trip's financial, logistical, and medical details. We used Doc's cabin upon our arrival, but shortly

Dr. Forgey's cabin was built in 1975. Upon our arrival in January, it was covered with snow. After spring thaw it became apparent a new roof was needed.

afterward built our own cabin some two miles away.

With so many things to consider, it took eighteen months for us to plan our dream adventure. Living in a wilderness log cabin for twelve months in the north country of Canada without electricity, plumbing, mail, telecommunications, or medical help is not to be taken lightly. As we planned our trip, our nutritional well-being was one of the many critical aspects that we couldn't ignore. To that end, we knew sourdough starter could prove vital in terms of our diets, and could provide much nutrition and energy. With sourdough, our diets wouldn't suffer.

On January 29, 1991, our goal approached reality when Dave and I chartered a 1956 single engine DeHavilland Otter bush plane to fly us—and our sourdough starter—to Doc Forgey's cabin 500 miles south of the Arctic Circle. The temperature that day reached 68-degrees below zero, the coldest day in twenty-five years.

While living in "the land God forgot," if we wanted bread we would have to make it ourselves. Fortunately, we planned well by bringing our sourdough starter, traditional stoneware crock, and a cookbook. All I had to do was follow the instructions, and everything else would "rise" into place, right? Wrong.

Sourdough cooking is tricky. It takes knowledge and practice to get it right. Once unpacked and settled into the cabin I began reading our sourdough cookbook, expecting to learn everything I needed to know. However, what I discovered were educational, but useless, details, such as the wheat kernel's three major parts (the endosperm, the embryo, and the bran) and that gluten flour is free of starch and produced from wheat flour, which is high in protein. All of these details were fascinating and insightful, but not practical. To make matters worse, most of the book's instructions were written for

Flying over the Little Beaver River in January, 1991. The cabin nestled somewhere in the trees below would be our home for the next twelve months.

As the plane flew away, leaving us to fend for ourselves, it dawned on me that I didn't know how to cook!

the ideal hometown kitchen. This was a problem, given my circumstances. Using my wood-burning stove I had no way of maintaining for any useful length of time the very warm room temperature recommended for getting the starter to ferment and the bread to proof. What I needed were practical nuts-'n-bolts

Top: *Our shelves loaded with some of the 1500 pounds of supplies we hauled in with us.* Bottom: *The formal dining room.*

Carefully stirring my sourdough starter ready to make even more breads!

details useful for my situation—baking while camping in the backcountry, sometimes at 40 degrees below zero.

Of course, the best things in the cookbook were the delicious recipes that, after working out the other tricky details, I eventually learned to transform into edible (sometimes even delicious) breads and pancakes.

On March 29, 1991, Doc Forgey arrived. He was our first visitor in three months and someone I could test my sourdough experiments on. Well, I suppose he enjoyed my experiments because as a consequence he encouraged me to write this book.

A lot has been written about sourdough, its folklore and its use. My intention with this book is to give you the information I needed while living at the cabin. My purpose is threefold: one, to inform you of the basics of successful sourdough cooking and baking while in the backcountry, where ideal baking circumstances are not found; two, by giving you a through knowledge of the basics to help alleviate the intimidation involved in using sourdough; three, to share with you some recipes that make sourdough cooking so rewarding.

I've tried to be conscientious about not including recipes that call for exotic ingredients such as kiwi, multicolored peppercorns, hemp, or ginseng root. Chances are you wouldn't take that stuff to a campout. But, if you do, great. Be sure to experiment and see what happens.

For me, this whole adventure in sourdough baking began in my wilderness home, the backwoods cabin. At times, back in civilization, I experience a thought, sight, or smell that instantly transports my mind back to that pristine place of natural phenomena and timelessness. The simplest thing can trigger the retrospection. In this case, it is the thought of baking with a wood stove that has brought memories—the smell, texture, and taste of the first successful loaf of bread I baked. One slice alone seemed a meal, but it was impossible to stop eating.

What a joy it was to be able to satisfy my taste buds with my own homemade (cabin made) bread. What seemed such an impossible task as baking bread (something only Grandma did), had become my own skill.

PART ONE

BEGINNING

Dave is quite the carpenter. He made this spice rack in just one day. We quickly began tacking recipes to the insides of the doors.

Chapter 1

Backcountry Baking Methods

IT WAS LATE JANUARY, 1991, the heart of winter, when Dave and I moved into Doc's wilderness cabin. For me, one of the many joys of our cabin life was the faithful wood-burning stove. Each frigid winter morning would begin with the building of a fire in the stove. This was done with the fervor of a ceremonial event, but not because of any ritualistic tradition—in the winter when the morning temperature is 40 degrees below zero Fahrenheit, warmth is the name of the game.

Once burning, the fire was fueled throughout the day. This made cooking and baking extremely convenient when it came time to try a new sourdough recipe. All I had to do was place my stovetop camp oven on the wood stove, put my dough inside, and let the baking begin. But as the cold winter season dwindled into the warmth of spring and summer, burning the wood stove became less necessary, thus baking on it became less practical. The result was different baking techniques.

From the writings of professional woodsmen such as Cliff Jacobson, Horace Kephart, and Calvin Rutstrum, I learned various ways to cook and bake. Fortunately, through trial and error I was able to customize their techniques to fit my circumstances.

How one bakes a recipe in the backcountry depends on a number of variables. First, your environment: you may be in a park where campfires are not permitted; second, your equipment: you may or may not have a reflector or Dutch oven, trail or wood stove; third, your personal preference and cooking style: the style you feel most competent with will yield the best results for you.

Whatever the situation may be, the three main sources of heat for baking in the bush are a campfire, a trail stove, and a wood stove. There are unique baking techniques that work well with each.

BAKING ON A CAMPFIRE

Baking on a campfire is a real test of skill and patience. It is perhaps the most difficult way to bake while camping because it requires a great deal of attention, time, and savvy for you to not burn the goods. Following are a few ways that you can bake over an open campfire. All techniques will require practice in order to perfect; don't be discouraged if your first attempt fails. Just keep trying and you will eventually master it and can impress your fellow campers.

The Reflector Oven

A reflector oven is excellent for turning out fine-tasting foods, but the secret of success is not in the oven, it's in the fire. When using a reflector oven, the fire must be high, bright, and hot.

Nowadays, the use of an open campfire for much more than roasting marshmallows or telling fireside stories has diminished, and so has the use of reflector ovens. Nevertheless, they work well.

When using a reflector oven, set it approximately eight inches away from the fire. Depending on what type of goods you are baking, you may be able to place the dough on the shelf itself; otherwise an appropriate baking tray will be needed. Regardless, make sure to grease whatever surface you place the bake goods on to help prevent sticking. To ensure the oven is heating and baking evenly, you may need to raise the base of the fire or build the

The reflector oven should be placed about eight inches away from the fire.

20

blaze upright, arranging the firewood in a pyramid. Baking times when using a reflector oven are about the same as when baking conventionally. The oven's open face allows visibility and quick access in case your food begins to scorch.

A couple of helpful hints: You'll need a metal spatula with a long handle to maneuver your breads. Also, it is necessary to keep the oven shiny for it to bake properly; Bon Ami cleanser works well for this.

Reflector ovens can be found at outdoor stores, Army-Navy stores, or Boy Scout outfitters. They are also easy to make. Several internet websites have directions—search for "reflector oven."

The Skillet Oven

"Bannock" is a Scottish Gaelic word for bread that can be cooked on a campfire. Typically, it is baked in a skillet. My recipe for Trailblazin' Bannock is on page 42.

To bake a bannock in a skillet on an open fire, grease the skillet well and spread the dough flat, about an inch thick. When the fire has burned down to a warm bed of coals, set the skillet on top. The baking process is slow, so patience is also a necessary ingredient.

Bake until the underside is golden brown, after which always shuffle the bannock until it is loose in the skillet, and flip it like a pancake. Bake the other side until it also is golden brown. To prevent burning the bannock and to help it bake evenly, you will need to rotate the skillet on the fire.

To test for doneness, either thump the bannock with your finger and listen for a hollow sound, or cut a sliver from the middle and taste test it. When it's done, it is best eaten while warm, but cooled bannocks keep well and make great trail snacks. Don't forget to embellish it with your favorite topping.

The Dutch Oven

For decades, Dutch ovens were commonplace in

To bake bannock, set the skillet on a bed of warm coals.

homes and "fixed" camps. But cooking with a Dutch oven may be a new skill for modern day campers.

The fact is, any traditional Dutch oven packed for use on the trail will not be convenient. That's because a traditional Dutch oven is made of ³⁄₁₆-inch-thick cast iron and can weigh up to 17 pounds. Its size and weight makes it completely impractical for use on typical camping and canoeing ventures. However, there's a Dutch oven made of cast aluminum that is more useful, lighter, and more compact. It should not be overlooked.

These ovens are excellent for baking and boiling. The top of the traditional Dutch oven has a handle, but a couple of manufacturers make them with a lid that also serves as a great skillet. Look for them at your local outdoor store or Boy Scout outfitter.

An aluminum Dutch oven doesn't need to be seasoned. However, with a cast iron one seasoning is necessary. Do this by coating the inside of the pot with cooking oil, and then baking it in an oven at 350 degrees for an hour or so.

Although my experience with Dutch oven cookery is limited to the aluminum ones, I have found that using a Dutch oven is easy, but of course cooking methods depend on your purpose.

Well-seasoned ovens need only a few drops of oil to prevent food from sticking. To bake in one, grease it, put your dough inside, and place the Dutch oven on a bed of hot coals. To prevent the food from burning, make sure the bottom of the oven is not directly on the coals, but elevated off them. If the oven doesn't have legs, elevate it with rocks or cover the

Left: *A traditional Dutch oven.* Right: *a Dutch oven incorporating a skillet with the lid.*

coals with ashes to help diffuse the heat. Pile hot coals on top of the oven, too, or maintain a small fire on top. When the main source of heat comes from the top there is a reduced chance of the food burning.

BAKING ON A TRAIL STOVE

At the cabin there were two trail stoves; one burned kerosene, the other white gas. Both worked well for baking. Being able to experiment with stoves that used two different kinds of fuel was insightful. With the diminishing use of open campfires for cooking, the popularity and use of trail stoves is great. Thus, it is necessary to be able to use them as efficiently and effectively as possible—unless you want to burn your buns! The trail stove baking method I used most was a spin-off of a technique called the triple-pan method. I call my spin-off the double-pan oven.

The Double-pan Oven

Place your dough in a well-greased, medium-sized saucepan without a handle. Put several small stones in the bottom of a larger pot. Let the dough proof, then place the saucepan with the dough inside the large pot. The space created by the small stones prevents burning. Leave the lid off the small pot, but cover the large one with a good-fitting lid or aluminum foil and place it on the stove

Baking bread with the double-pan oven. A few small stones on the bottom of the larger pot creates space to prevent burning.

over low heat. This procedure takes a while for baking, but yields good results. It can also be used over the campfire.

The Jell-O® Mold Oven

Cliff Jacobson, in his book *Camping Secrets*, describes a technique for trail stove baking called the Jell-O® Mold Oven. Due to my not having a Jell-O® mold, I was unable to try this. In his book, Cliff writes:

All you need is a large ring aluminum Jell-O® mold (under $10 at most discount stores or on the internet) and a high cover. To use the mold for baking on your stove:

1. Grease the mold and pour your bake stuff into the outside ring. Decrease the suggested amount of water by up to 25 percent for faster baking.

2. Bring the stove to its normal operating temperature, then reduce the heat to its lowest possible blue flame setting. Center the mold over the burner head, top it with a high cover (essential to provide room for the bread to rise), and relax. Heat goes up the chimney of the mold, radiates off the cover, and cooks from the top, with no chance of burning.

3. Cool the mold by setting it in a shallow pan of water for a few moments. *Important:* Even a light breeze will cause uneven heating of the Jell-O® mold, resulting in a cake that has one side burned and one side raw. So rotate the mold frequently

The Jell-O® mold oven is a unique technique for baking on a trail stove.

to distribute heat evenly. A windscreen of some sort is essential when using a Jell-O® Mold Oven.

BAKING ON A WOOD STOVE

I've saved wood-stove baking to talk about last because it's so simple and hassle free. It is my favorite method of baking, and in my opinion is the finest.

If a wood stove is being used, chances are the setting is in a cabin or "fixed" camp. Wood stoves are sometimes designed with an oven compartment for baking. If you are using one of these stoves, great—no instructions are needed except to tell you to check your food periodically for burning. With an oven compartment, the baking procedure is rather conventional.

If the wood stove is similar to the one I am accustomed to, the fire burns inside the stove while cooking takes place on the top. If this is the case, using a stovetop camp oven or Dutch oven produces good results.

In the summer, I used a wood stove outside to bake bread. Otherwise it would become too hot inside the cabin. The first (and last) time I baked bread in the cabin during the summer, the candles melted!

The Stovetop Camp Oven

This piece of equipment is wonderfully convenient. Just set the oven on top of the wood stove to preheat, and once it is heated place the pan with its breadstuff inside the oven. Make sure to keep a hot fire going in the wood stove, but not an inferno.

Some stovetop camp ovens come with a temperature gauge on the outside. This is handy, but it is not always accurate. Keep a close eye so you don't burn your food. Stovetop camp ovens are available through camping outfitters or on the internet. The most commonly used camp oven is manufactured by Coleman, and sells for $30 to $40, new. It measures about a foot all around, weighs seven pounds, and can be folded for transport.

The stovetop camp oven is convenient for baking on a woodstove.

The Dutch Oven

The use of the Dutch oven on a campfire was described on pages 22-23. The same directions apply here; the only difference is that you will need to place the Dutch oven inside the wood stove, piling hot coals on top. Be careful not to burn the bottom, and remember to elevate the Dutch oven off the bottom coals.

Chapter 2

Making Sourdough

THIS BOOK PROVIDES YOU with the basics of successful sourdough cooking and baking while in the backcountry, where ideal cooking conditions are not found. In this chapter I share helpful hints regarding the utensils, ingredients, and special instructions necessary for successful sourdough cooking.

INGREDIENTS

An acquaintance of mine is a professional chef. He has prepared dishes for people such as the first President George Bush and fashion designer Ralph Lauren. One evening while we were at a social gathering, my chef friend told me about the importance of using high quality ingredients. He said the final product of any recipe is only as good as the lowest quality ingredient. However, in my case, in the backcountry high quality ingredients are not always available, unless, of course, that's what you brought with you. When I purchased the groceries for my stay at the cabin the quantity of supplies was more important to me than the quality.

So there I was, in my cabin, with mediocre ingredients and the advice of a professional chef, which I could not follow. However, I did have the one thing that made up for this terrible loss—hunger. When you're hungry in the backcountry, the finest ingredients couldn't make that much of a difference because all you want to do is eat—a lot!

In this book I've avoided any recipes that call for swanky ingredients you most likely wouldn't take along. You won't find things such as pralines, candied cherries, or ginseng root in the following recipes. But let's talk about some of the basic ingredients you will find.

If you are buying your supplies for a long camping trip, it can be expensive!

Flour

In addition to sourdough, which is the leavening agent, flour is one of the most important ingredients. There are many types of flour available on the market, from sources such as wheat, rye, yellow or white corn, barley, buckwheat, oats, peanuts, soy, rice, potatoes, and various combinations of grains. Among wheat flours there is white all-purpose (both bleached and unbleached), cake, self-rising (not recommended for sourdough cooking), whole wheat, gluten, and seminola.

Most of the flours listed above are "exotic" ingredients, and you won't need them for any recipes in this book. The flours called for in this book include white or all-purpose, whole wheat, and rye.

White all-purpose flour. The best flour to use for these recipes is unbleached, hard white wheat. All-purpose flour is made from a combination of ground hard and soft wheat. Typically, when using all-purpose flour for breads, the result is lighter, moist bread. When using it for cakes, I have found sifting the flour a few times first makes a more crumbly cake. I used all-purpose flour in every recipe; it's all I had, but it worked very well.

Whole Wheat Flour. The best whole wheat flour has been stone ground. This is slower to spoil.

Rye Flour. When using rye flour you will get stickier, more elastic dough. Also, if you are allergic to wheat, rye is an adequate replacement.

When storing flour, try to find a cool dry place that's mouse free. In camp I had delinquent mice that enjoyed vandalizing my flour; you may have them too. Also, stir your flour before measuring it to remove any lumps so your measurements are correct. This also eliminates the need for sifting.

Leaveners

There are two main categories of leaveners: yeasts and chemical leaveners.

Yeast. Commercially produced yeast, which is sold in grocery stores, is used as a basis for your fresh sourdough starter. Packaged dry sourdough starter is also a type of yeast. Either will work. Some people who make sourdough rely on wild yeasts that are in the air and in flour. However, to give your sourdough a reliable start, use commercial yeast. Since yeast is a living organism (actually, a type of fungus), regular feedings of flour and water will keep it alive indefinitely.

With the combination of yeast, flour, water, and warmth, the yeast micro-organisms reproduce, and as they do, they ferment the natural sugar that is present in the flour. In this process, carbon dioxide bubbles are given off, causing bread to rise and making it light and fluffy. Along with the yeast is naturally occurring, acid-generating bacteria, which give the starter its sour flavor. These, too, multiply as the sourdough ages. So there it is: Sourdough starter is a fungus and some bacteria . . . and it makes delicious bread!

If your starter becomes discolored or foul smelling it has been contaminated. Throw it out and make new starter.

Chemical Leaveners. The two most popular chemical leaveners are baking soda and baking powder. These can be added to ensure the bread's ability to rise. However, neither will increase sourdough's sour flavor.

I give a recipe for Trailblazin' Bannock on page 42, in which you can substitute baking powder for the primary batter if necessary or desired. Replace the 2 cups of batter with 2 tablespoons of baking powder and 1 cup of water. You won't have the sour flavor, but it does taste good and has been fixed and eaten

Bannock is a skillet bread that is very easy to make, either on a wood stove, as pictured, or over a campfire.

in the backcountry by campers for decades. As a matter of fact, when I was in the main terminal of the Thompson, Manitoba, airport, waiting to board the 1956 single engine Otter bush plane that was taking me to the cabin, a security guard, an older Frenchman, upon hearing where I was going asked me, "Do ya know how to make bannock?" He asked his question with urgency, the kind that comes only from knowing something someone else needs to know. Happy to see his genuine concern, I replied, "Oh, yes I do!"

Sweeteners

Sweeteners are fun ingredients. By substituting one kind for another you can alter the flavor of your product. For example, try substituting brown sugar, molasses, or honey for white sugar. Each gives your recipe a different taste.

Be careful to add the correct amount of sugar, honey, or other sweetener. When used in larger amounts, sweeteners will slow the action of the sourdough. Also, do not use artificial sweeteners, because many of them become bitter when the recipe is cooked.

Also, try baking soda as a sweetener, for it acts against the acid that puts the sour in sourdough. However, be careful to add the soda at the very last moment before baking; this helps prevent the leavening characteristics of the soda from affecting the leavening of the sourdough.

Fats

The best fat to use is butter. It can be replaced by an equal amount of margarine or shortening, but they do alter the taste.

Egg Substitute

Here is a suggestion for the following recipes that you may find peculiar. If you don't have eggs while camping in the snow, for every egg called for in a recipe, use 1 cup of snow. The snow has the same effect that eggs do, giving the recipe the necessary consistency. This may sound crazy, but it works, and has been used by generations of woodsmen and prospectors alike.

CONTAINERS FOR SOURDOUGH

The success of any sourdough recipe depends a great deal on using the correct utensils. However, when in the woods you don't always have what you need. That's fine—use what you've got. Not using the correct utensils won't completely ruin your product. I just want to offer some guidelines that will help ensure the superiority of your final goodie.

Calvin Rutstrum, the famous woodsman, once told a story about a device he made in which to carry his starter. It was designed like a crock, but he installed a valve on the lid so that when the gases built up the valve would open, letting them escape. Unfortunately, when he packed it away in his Duluth pack the starter obstructed the valve, not allowing it to open. While portaging the pack, the massive explosion of the container knocked Cal off his feet, pitching him flat on his face. He said it was as if someone had kicked him in the back with a giant foot. Everything in his pack was covered with sourdough!

The best containers for your sourdough starter are either a traditional stoneware crock or a plastic container made by companies such as Rubbermaid or Tupperware. As to weight and durability, I've found a plastic container is the best. It is light and easy to deal with and won't break when packed. It does however, lack the sense of antiquity that a stoneware crock possesses. Whether or not antiquity is of any value while in the bush is debatable. I suggest that if you decide to use a stoneware crock, be sure to remove the rubber seal that comes with it. This is so the sourdough can breathe, and the gases produced by the starter can escape. If you don't remove the seal, gases will build up inside the crock until it literally explodes. If you use a plastic container, puncture small holes in the lid with a nail to prevent its exploding.

When on the trail, there are two convenient and hassle-free ways to carry your sourdough:

Take about ½ cup of starter and add flour until it's a soft, pliable ball of dough. Generously sprinkle the dough with more flour and put it in a plastic bag filled halfway with flour. Seal the bag well and the starter should last a week or two. When you're ready to use it, remove the sourdough from the bag. Leave any loose flour in the bag for reuse. Place the sourdough in a mixing bowl. Add 2 cups of water, 2 cups of flour, and let it sit in a warm place for at least 3 hours, after which it will be ready to use in any recipe.

A second way of carrying sourdough is to dry it. A couple nights before your trip, take a piece of waxed paper and lay it flat across a table. Then take about ½ cup or more of sourdough starter and spread it across the paper. Let it dry until it is brittle. Break it up into pieces and put them into a container. When the sourdough is needed, just add small amounts of water at a time to rehydrate into batter.

SPECIAL INSTRUCTIONS

Here are a few special things you should know to help you succeed with sourdough:

- Do not leave your sourdough in contact with metal for a long time. Aluminum and copper will drastically react with your sourdough and affect its flavor. However, stainless steel utensils are fine to use.
- Remember, sourdough is a leavener. It can cause your batter to double or triple in bulk. Be sure to use containers large enough to handle the expansion.
- When it comes to the clean up after the preparation of any sourdough recipe, heed these words: *clean your dishes immediately after their use!* If

you do, you can't go wrong. If you don't, then be aware that there is no way to calculating exactly how many years it may take you to get those dishes clean. It may take only months if you use a hammer and chisel!

SOURDOUGH STARTERS AND BATTERS

To make any sourdough recipe, you need two things, sourdough starter and primary batter.

You must begin with a *sourdough starter*. This is what you keep in your sourdough crock. It is sacred, and you must never let it run out. As long as you have starter, you can make sourdough recipes. You must always replenish your starter as you use it to make your primary batter for the recipes.

Primary batter is made from your starter. Every recipe in this book calls for it. The batter is the leavening agent, the most important ingredient and foundation of every recipe in this book.

There are two methods for obtaining sourdough starter: commercial starter and homemade starter.

Commercial Starter

Commercially produced starters cost around $4 to $5 and can be purchased at your local grocer or from various camp outfitters.

Typically, commercial starters come in ½-ounce packages of dry culture, and include instructions on preparing the starter. The dry culture is combined with 2 cups of flour and 2 cups of warm (not hot) water. Mix with a wooden or plastic spoon. After this, cover your starter container tightly with a plastic wrap and let it rest in a warm (not hot) draft-free place for 36 to 48 hours. Depending on the temperature, it may take a few hours more or less.

During the winter months in the cabin the temperature was rarely warm enough, long enough time to allow the starter to develop. To remedy the problem, I wrapped the starter in extra blankets or something of the like to keep it insulated. You may need to do the same.

After enough time has passed, the starter should appear bubbly and smell sour. Some have said the sour smell is similar to that of beer. The consistency of the starter will be the same as that of thin pancake batter.

At this point, your commercial starter is ready to use. From it, you can make the primary batter necessary for any sourdough recipe. You will need to keep the starter in a container that will withstand sourdough's properties, as mentioned on pages 31–32. Until you're ready to make the primary batter for a recipe, store the starter in a cool place.

Homemade Starter

If you would rather make your own starter, it's simple to do. Mix 2 cups of flour with 1 tablespoon sugar and ½ cake of yeast. Then add warm water and stir until it resembles thin pancake batter. Let the mixture sit uncovered at room temperature for 36 to 48 hours until it sours. The old woodsman axiom is "the sourer the better." So the longer it sits, the more sour it smells, and the better it will taste. This is true of commercial starters as well. The sour effect of homemade starter is dependent upon an appropriate bacteria level.

PRIMARY BATTER

As the name implies, the starter is only the beginning. From the starter you will make the key ingredient of all sourdough recipes: primary batter. Whether you are using a commercial or homemade starter, the process for making your primary batter is the same.

The batter needs to be made well in advance of its use, approximately 8 to 12 hours ahead of time. To make the batter, combine ½ cup of starter with ½ cup flour and 1 cup warm water. Add only enough water to make a thin batter. Typically, 1 cup warm water works fine, but depending on the flour used, you may need more or less water.

After mixing the ingredients, cover your bowl of batter and let it proof in a warm, draft-free area for 8 to 12 hours. Once the batter has proofed, it will look bubbly and smell sour. At this point it is ready to use. Measure out the amount of primary batter needed for the recipe. Put any leftover batter back into the container of original starter.

After removing a portion of the starter to make batter, it is necessary for you to rejuvenate your starter to keep it living. To do this, simply replace what you took with equal amounts of flour and warm water. For example, if you measured out 1 cup of starter, replace it with 1 cup of flour and 1 cup of warm water. This will help ensure the longevity of your starter, keeping it fresh and useful.

PART TWO

RECIPES

Here I am preparing to make some bread by portioning out my primary batter.

Chapter 3

Appetizers

- Boonie Bread Sticks   37
- Pretzels   39
- Salt Crackers   39
- Scottish Scones   40
- Wild Wheat Crackers   40

BOONIE BREAD STICKS

Yields 30 bread sticks

1½ cups primary batter
1 cup hot water
3 tablespoons butter or margarine
3 tablespoons sugar
1 teaspoon salt
4 cups flour

Mix the ingredients in order, as listed. Add the flour slowly, ½ cup at a time. Knead the dough on a flat surface, adding additional flour until the dough is elastic. Place the dough in a greased plastic container and let it sit for 2 hours for proofing, after which, roll out to a ½-inch thickness and cut the dough into strips no wider than 1 inch. Place the strips on a greased baking sheet, at least 1 inch apart. Bake for 20 minutes at 400 degrees, or until golden brown.

One of the funniest times of my stay at the cabin was all about oleo. Oleo? What, you've never heard of it? Me either. That's what is so amusing about this story.

On February 4, 1991, Dave Scott, my partner, found a cookbook full of delicious-sounding recipes. It described all sorts of goodies such as backwoods lasagna and chocolate cake. Every important backcountry recipe one would want was in this little old recipe book that suddenly became our hungry bellies' best friend. Dave and I were elated, but there was a problem. All the recipes contained an ingredient we hadn't heard of, called "oleo."

The closest Dave and I had ever come to oleo was Oreo, as in the cookie. It crossed our minds that maybe this was a typo. Maybe the ingredient was meant to be Oreo instead of oleo. But of course not. Who would want to put ½ cup of Oreos in a dish of Fettuccini Alfredo?

We looked in the dictionary for a definition and we consulted other books we had available, but not one of them said anything about oleo. And, being over a hundred miles away from the nearest town, there was no one we could ask.

What to do? Theoretically, we could have hiked out on snowshoes, but that wasn't practical for something that might be a typo. There we were, with a well-earned hunger, a recipe book of savory foods to feed on, but no oleo.

We decided not to worry about it, and just try to work around it. Besides, we still had other recipes up our collective sleeve. If, and when, we had a visitor from the outside we would simply ask them about oleo. Hopefully, they'd know the answer.

Two months later that same year we had our first visitor from the outside, none other than our mentor, bearer of news, current events, and nutritional trivia, Doc Forgey. Among all the things that were on our minds to ask about, such as how were our families, what about the Persian Gulf War, and how "da" Chicago Bulls were doing, a question with high priority was, what the hell is oleo?

"Oleo is an old-fashioned term for margarine," Doc answered "Why do you ask?"

Dave and I just looked at each other, feeling the effect of our youth. We had oleo the whole time, and lots of it. It was in the container labeled butter! Needless to say, Doc got a great laugh out of that one.

PRETZELS
Yields 15 4-inch wide pretzels

1½ cups primary batter
1 cup hot water
3 tablespoons melted butter or margarine
3 tablespoons sugar
2½ teaspoons salt
5½ cups flour
1 egg or 1 cup snow
2 tablespoons milk

Mix the ingredients in order, as listed. Add the flour slowly, ½ cup at a time. Knead the dough on a flat surface for about 5 minutes. Let the dough rest for 2 hours to proof. Break off the dough in pieces about the size of a handball, roll each of the pieces into a 15-inch length, and shape them into your favorite pretzel shape. Place the pretzels on a greased baking sheet or griddle, and set in a warm place for 20 to 30 minutes for proofing. Sprinkle with salt and bake at 425 degrees for 15 minutes or until browned. Let cool, then serve.

SALT CRACKERS
Yields about 50 crackers

2 tablespoons shortening
2 teaspoons salt
½ cup primary batter
1 cup white flour

Mix the ingredients in order, as listed. Knead the dough and add some white flour until it becomes just stiff. Roll the dough out very thin and cut into 2-inch squares. Place the squares on a greased baking sheet or griddle. Pierce each square with a fork and sprinkle with more salt. Bake at 400 degrees for 5 to 10 minutes or until the crackers begin to brown. Let cool completely before serving.

SCOTTISH SCONES
Yields 10 scones

1 cup primary batter
2½ tablespoons sugar
½ teaspoon salt
1 teaspoon baking soda
¼ cup melted butter
1 egg or 1 cup snow
1 cup white flour

Mix the ingredients in order, as listed. Add the flour slowly. The dough should be thick, but easy to work with. The less kneading you do, the flakier the scone will be. Place a heaping tablespoon of the batter into a hot greased frying pan over medium heat. Cook until the underside is brown, then flip and cook until the other side is brown. Serve hot with butter and jam.

WILD WHEAT CRACKERS
Yields about 75 crackers

2 cups whole wheat flour
1 teaspoon dill seeds
1 teaspoon salt
½ cup shortening
1 cup primary batter

Mix the ingredients in order, as listed. Knead thoroughly to bring out the gluten to make a thinner cracker. Place the dough on a floured board and roll it very, very thin. Cut into 2-inch squares and put the squares on a greased baking sheet or griddle. Pierce the squares with a fork and bake at 375 degrees for 30 minutes or until brown.

Chapter 4

Breads, Rolls & Biscuits

- Trailblazin' Bannock   42
- Biscuits   42
- Bread Rolls   44
- Cheddar Cheese Bread   44
- Country Cornbread   45
- English Muffins   45
- No-knead Bread   46
- No-knead Cornmeal-Raisin Bread   46
- No-knead Colonial Bread   47
- No-knead Peanut Butter Bread   47
- Oatmeal Raisin Cakes   48
- Raisin Muffins   48
- Scott's Cabin Bread   49
- French Bread   49
- French Rolls   51

SOURDOUGH BREAD. Ah, that porous wonder! The kind of wonder that, in and of itself, is more than meets the eye. To wit, when I make bread I don't just see the culmination of some ingredients thrown together. I see beyond the obvious and look for some peanut butter and jelly to make a PB&J sandwich.

Bread is much more than the simple sum of its ingredients. Bread is the foundation of the seven epicurean wonders of the world: French toast, grilled cheese sandwiches, peanut butter and jelly sandwiches, pizza crust, garlic bread, bologna sandwiches, and cinnamon toast. White, whole wheat, rye, or pumpernickel, it doesn't really matter. All of these gratifying edible delights are obtainable only with bread.

TRAILBLAZIN' BANNOCK
Yields 1 loaf

This is the recipe that a wise-looking security guard in the Thompson, Manitoba, Canada airport lobby asked me about. "Do ya know how to make bannock?" he queried upon hearing that I was traveling to a remote wilderness cabin for a year.

Bannock is superlative for treks, and campouts. It's easy to prepare, requires no proofing time, and there is no baking. This bread is fried in a skillet like a pancake; some call it skillet bread.

 2 cups primary batter
 ½ cup butter
 1 teaspoon salt
 1 tablespoon sugar
 1 cup flour

Mix the dry ingredients, then stir in the batter. Mix well until the dough is like a thick pancake batter. Pour dough into a warm, lightly greased skillet. Fry until the underside is done, then flip it to cook the other side. When both sides are golden brown, serve. See page 21 for more about cooking bannock.

BISCUITS
Yields 10 to 15 biscuits

 1½ cups primary batter
 1 cup flour
 ½ teaspoon salt
 1 tablespoon sugar
 ¼ cup melted butter

Mix the ingredients in order, as listed. Pour the dough onto a floured surface and knead no more than 1 minute. The less you knead, the flakier the biscuits will be. Roll out to ½-inch thickness. Using a cookie cutter or knife, cut out the biscuits and place them on a greased pie pan or baking sheet. Brush the tops with butter. Let them sit in a warm place for 30 minutes or until double in bulk. Bake at 375 degrees for 30 minutes or until golden brown.

L ife in the backcountry is sometimes rough, but always rewarding. I believe there is no reason to limit the experience with a diet of nuts and berries. You need bread.

Forget about trying to pack in store-bought bread—it's a hassle. Besides, it'll never make the trip without getting smashed into bits. Impress your trip partners, impress yourself, and show your culinary skill by baking bread while in the woods. When the loaf is done baking, cut a hot slice, spread butter on it, close your eyes, and enjoy. You'll eat until you're full or until it's all gone, whichever comes first. So, don't be an unleavened person. Live a full life and celebrate it with sourdough, the superhero of leaveners, the friend of adventurers and prospectors throughout history.

Furthermore, sourdough causes magical things to occur. Things that you don't expect. Things that will cause you to give thanks. A personal experience of this came one day while at the cabin. I was preparing a loaf of sourdough rye bread when I heard the alluring sound of a flying machine in the distance. I was very excited, hoping it would be someone flying in to visit.

Stopping what I was doing, I rushed outside to look for the plane and the potential visitor. Much to my dismay, it was just a helicopter flying very fast in the western horizon, heading north to Churchill. Very disappointed, I went back into the cabin to finish baking my bread. A short while later I heard the sound again, this time quite close. Once again, my heart pounded from the possibility of having human visitors.

I ran outside and my wish was granted. This time, instead of the helicopter being far off in the horizon, it was directly above the cabin, so close I could see the eyes of the passengers inside. Startled, yet elated, I waved calmly to appear cautious. Seconds later the pilot landed the helicopter on the river bank. Out of it jumped a bearded man whom I had never seen. In that intense moment, many questions flooded my mind. Who were they? Why were they here? Where had they come from? Was there trouble? Was this friend or foe?

For the sake of congeniality, I approached the stranger with my hand extended, and we shook hands. The first words spoken by the man rang in my ears as proof of sourdough's magical properties.

"Heard there was a bakery around here," he said. Dumbfounded and relieved, I smiled big and invited them in for fresh baked bread and coffee. For the next hour, we visited, laughed, and they told us of current events back in civilization. Arriving as strangers, they left as friends.

BREAD ROLLS
Yields 10 to 15 rolls

1½ cups primary batter
1 tablespoon sugar
½ teaspoon salt
2 tablespoons melted butter
1 egg or 1 cup snow
2 cups flour of your choice

Mix the ingredients in order, as listed. Add the flour a bit at a time. Mix until the dough is smooth, then knead the dough on a flat floured surface. If needed, add additional flour for elasticity. Place the dough back into a bowl and put it in a warm place until double in bulk. Punch it down and continue to let it sit until double in bulk again. Once done, roll dough out to ½ inch thickness, and cut into pieces about 3 inches in diameter. Form the pieces into rolls, and place them on a greased baking sheet. Let sit for 30 minutes, then bake them at 400 degrees for 15 to 20 minutes, or until golden brown.

CHEDDAR CHEESE BREAD
Yields 1 loaf

1½ cups primary batter
1 cup milk
¼ cup sugar
1 teaspoon salt
3 tablespoons melted butter
1 egg or 1 cup snow
2 cups grated cheddar cheese
4 cups white flour

Mix the ingredients in order, as listed. Add the flour a little at a time. Once the ingredients are mixed, turn the dough out onto a flat, floured surface and knead it until it is soft. Form into a loaf and place it in a greased bread pan. Let it sit in a warm place until double in bulk. Bake at 375 degrees for 30 minutes or until golden brown. Test for doneness by thumping the loaf with your finger and listen for a hollow sound. Remove the bread from the pan and let it cool.

COUNTRY CORNBREAD
Yields 1 loaf

1½ cups primary batter
1½ cups yellow cornmeal
1 cup milk
2 eggs or 2 cups snow
2 tablespoons sugar
½ cup melted butter
½ teaspoons salt

Stir the ingredients together and pour the batter into a greased bread pan. Bake at 450 degrees for 25 minutes or until golden brown. This bread is complete only when served hot with lots of butter.

ENGLISH MUFFINS
Yields 10 muffins

1½ cups primary batter
1½ cups flour
1 tablespoon sugar
½ teaspoons salt

Mix the ingredients in order, as listed. Knead the dough on a flat floured surface until the dough is easy to handle without being sticky. Roll the dough out to a thickness of ½-inch. Using a knife or cookie cutter, cut out the muffins. Put each muffin on a greased baking sheet about an inch apart and sprinkle with cornmeal. Let them rest in a warm place for an hour to proof. Cook the muffins for 10 minutes on each side in a greased frying pan. Serve hot or let cool to be eaten later.

NO-KNEAD BREAD
Yields 1 loaf

1½ cups primary batter
½ cup milk
1 teaspoon salt
2 tablespoons sugar
2 tablespoons cooking oil or shortening
3 cups flour

Mix the dry ingredients first, then add the batter. Mix well. Once the dough is mixed, form a loaf or just pour the dough into a greased pan. Bake immediately until golden brown, or test for doneness by thumping the loaf with your finger. If you hear a hollow sound the bread is done. Remove the bread from the pan and let it cool.

NO-KNEAD CORNMEAL-RAISIN BREAD
Yields 2 loaves

3 cups primary batter
¼ cup melted shortening
1½ cups milk
¾ cup brown sugar
2 teaspoons salt
2 eggs or 2 cups snow
2 teaspoons cinnamon
1½ cups yellow cornmeal
4 cups white flour
2 cups raisins

Mix the ingredients in order, as listed, but slowly. Be sure to add the flour a little at a time, stirring after each addition. Mix until the batter is stiff. Put it in a warm place for 2 hours to proof or until double in bulk. After the proofing is done, stir the batter again. Put the batter in two greased bread pans, and let proof again until double in bulk. Bake at 375 degrees for 45 minutes or until golden brown. When done, remove the loaves from the pans to cool.

NO-KNEAD COLONIAL BREAD
Yields 1 loaf

1½ cups primary batter
½ cup milk
1 tablespoon sugar
½ teaspoon salt
½ cup raisins
½ cup nuts
1½ cups flour

Mix dry ingredients first, then add the batter. Mix well. Allow dough to stay soft. Pour dough into a greased pan, cover, and let sit in a warm place for an hour. Bake for 1 hour or until done.

NO-KNEAD PEANUT BUTTER BREAD
Yields 1 loaf

1½ cups primary batter
½ cup brown sugar
½ cup milk
¾ cups melted peanut butter
½ teaspoon salt
2 tablespoons melted butter
2½ cups wheat flour

Mix the ingredients in order, as listed. Add the flour a little at a time. Once mixed, pour the batter into the bread pan and let it sit in a warm place for 30 minutes. Bake at 350 degrees for 45 minutes or until done. Remove the loaf from the pan and let it cool.

OATMEAL RAISIN CAKES
Yields 6 cakes

1 cup primary batter
2 tablespoons sugar
½ teaspoon salt
¼ cup melted butter
2 eggs or 2 cups snow
½ cup raisins
1 cup oats (rolled or quick-cooking—whatever you've got)
¾ cup white flour

Mix the ingredients well. Knead the dough on a flat floured surface until dough holds together. Divide the dough into six pieces or cakes. Place them on a greased baking sheet and let them sit in a warm place for an hour. Before baking, cut slits in the top of each cake. Bake at 400 degrees for 20 minutes or until the cakes are brown. Best when served warm.

RAISIN MUFFINS
Yields 8 to 12 muffins

1½ cups primary batter
1½ cups flour
3 tablespoons brown sugar
½ teaspoon salt
¼ cup shortening
1 egg or 1 cup snow
1 cup raisins

Mix the ingredients in order, as listed. The dough should be moist and lumpy. Put the dough in a greased muffin pan with individual cups and let it rest in a warm place for proofing until double in bulk. Bake at 400 degrees for 25 minutes or until done.

SCOTT'S CABIN BREAD
Yields 2 loaves

Below is the recipe that prompted me to write this book. This bread recipe became an icon of survival and a mealtime favorite. Typically, I made white bread, among others, at least three times a week. Good old white bread seemed to be the quickest and became the favorite to fix.

The recipe got its name for obvious reasons. It didn't seem fair to limit its name to Sourdough Bread. How boring—and besides, too many inhabitants of too many cabins, both past and present, have been fed from the sourdough crock to leave out the word "cabin" from its name.

> 3 cups primary batter
> 2 tablespoons melted butter
> ⅓ cup sugar
> 1 teaspoon salt
> 2½ cups white or all-purpose flour

Mix dry ingredients first, then add the batter. Mix well. Pour the dough onto a floured surface and knead. Once the dough is consistently elastic, form your loaf by rolling it up in layers like a jellyroll, adding flour if needed. Place the loaf in a greased bread pan. Set in a warm place for 2 hours or until double in bulk. After proofing, bake it at 400 degrees for 30 minutes until golden brown, or test for doneness by thumping the loaf with your finger. If you hear a hollow sound, the bread is done.

FRENCH BREAD
Yields 2 loaves

> 1½ cups primary batter
> 1 cup warm water
> 2 teaspoons salt
> 4 cups flour

Combine the primary batter and the warm water (no hotter than 95 degrees) in a large bowl. Stir in 1 cup of flour and spread the salt on the top of the batter. Mix in the additional flour ½ cup at a time. While mixing, scrape the sides of the bowl so the dough doesn't stick. Use additional flour if necessary. Pour the dough onto a well floured flat surface and knead it until the dough is smooth and elastic, adding flour if needed. Place the dough in a large, warm bowl at least 4 quarts in capacity. Cover tightly with plastic wrap and place in a warm spot for proofing. This should take 2 hours, or until double in size.

After the dough has doubled in size, knead it on a lightly floured surface for about a minute, and divide the dough into 2 equal pieces. Fold each piece in half lengthwise, cover, and let them rest for 5 minutes. Each piece can be shaped into a loaf by patting it out into a large oval about 1½ inches thick. Fold each loaf from back to front and seal the near edge by pinching it in several places. Roll the dough around so the seal is on the top. With your hands, flatten the dough again and press a trench down the center of the oval with your fingers. Fold the pieces in half lengthwise again and seal the near edge again by pinching it. Then roll the dough back and forth in the palms of your hands until it reaches a length about 2 inches shorter than your baking sheet.

Once the loaves are the right size, put them on a greased baking sheet that has been covered with white cornmeal. Be sure to place the loaves at least 3

Don't get your hopes up on being able to bake sourdough French bread that tastes like what you get in San Francisco. It just won't happen. Why? Because the main ingredient can't be bought in any store, anywhere, not even in San Francisco. It's called Lactobacillus sanfrancisco, *a bacterium exclusive to the Bay area. In San Francisco, as the bread proofs, a sugar called maltose is made. The bacterium uses the maltose to make lactic and acetic acids, 70 and 30 percent respectively. This gives the bread its sour flavor.*

We must call a spade a spade. Even if we had Lactobacillus sanfrancisco, *we still don't have the expertise and special equipment necessary to produce the world famous sourdough French bread that the Bay City master bakers create. However, we must rise to the occasion of a backcountry French bread feast and put our best recipes to the test. And, if that doesn't work, there's an old fable that claims old-time bakers gave the bread its special flavor by shaping the dough and making the loaves in their armpits. Try this and taste what happens. It may work. If all else fails, you may find out that your dough makes better deodorant.*

inches apart from each other, with the seam down. Cover the loaves with a cloth, but don't let the covering touch the dough. Put in a warm place for proofing until double in bulk. This will probably take 1 hour, after which the loaves are ready to bake. Before putting them in the oven, cut three diagonal slashes across the top of each loaf, then brush them with cold water. The cuts and cold water help to give the crust its rough texture and golden color.

Put a pan of water in the bottom of the preheated oven. This produces steam and helps brown the crust. Bake the loaves in the oven at 400 degrees. After 10 minutes of baking, remove the pan of water and continue to bake the loaves for 35 minutes or until they are browned. Remove the loaves and let them cool on a wire rack. To add sheen to the crust, brush with water. Avoid the temptation to eat the bread while it's hot and smells so good. French bread is not done baking until the bread has completely cooled. It tastes much better that way.

FRENCH ROLLS
Yields 15 rolls

1½ cups primary batter
1 cup warm water
2 teaspoons salt
4 cups flour

Follow the directions above for sourdough French bread until the proofing is completed. After the dough has doubled in size, turn it onto a flat floured surface and knead it for 1 minute, then roll it out flat to a 1½ inch thickness. With a sharp knife or cookie cutter cut the dough into 15 pieces, each 4 inches square.

Fold each piece over itself and seal the edge by pinching it. Put the rolls on a greased baking sheet that has been covered with white cornmeal. Place the rolls in rows about 3 inches apart. Cover the dough with a cloth, but don't let it touch the rolls, and set them in a warm spot until double in bulk. Before baking, cut a lengthwise slash in each roll with a sharp knife and brush the rolls with cold water.

Preheat the oven to 400 degrees and put a pan of boiling water on the bottom. Place the rolls in the oven. Bake for 15 minutes and remove the pan of water. Continue to bake the rolls for an additional 30 minutes or until golden brown. Remove the rolls and let them cool on wire racks.

Chapter 5

Entrees

- Country Fry Batter   53
- Papa's Noobles   53
- Pizza Crust   54
- Dumplings   55

Decades ago, sourdough was equivalent to the American Express card—you didn't leave home without it. Inside a crock of zesty, bubbling sourdough starter was the potential for mouth watering breads, biscuits, pancakes, and even entrees, all while on the trail.

Nowadays, in an age of high-tech quick-fix, dehydrated, silver bag entrees like Turkey Tetrazzini and Cantonese Shrimp, who wants to deal with a messy, bubbling ooze that smells sour and could blow up in your pack at any time unless properly stored? Who could possibly be crazy enough to pack a thing like sourdough?

Me.

During our stint in Canada, Dave and I experimented with our choices for dinner entrees. Yes, we did bring our ration of high-tech trail food, the choice of astronauts, tech weenies, and yuppies everywhere. Yes, trail food is convenient, lightweight, easy to fix, and relatively tasty, and we ate our share of it. But don't be fooled. We did not use trail food instead of sourdough, but in addition to sourdough, which gave us some variety. And for that we're thankful. However, one package of trail food is only good for one meal, whereas one package of sourdough is good for hundreds of meals, generations of hungry bellies, and it can choke starvation to death.

ENTREES ARE USUALLY ASSOCIATED with dinner. After a long, hard day of trekking or canoeing, the thought of a hearty-flavored dinner is overwhelming. The choice of just the right entree is crucial. For Dave and me, pizza was usually the choice. We loved to whip up some sourdough pizza dough and make "za" anytime we were feeling really hungry. Pizza is usually well accepted among varied campers, which makes it a good menu choice on trips, so be sure to try the pizza dough recipe on page 54.

COUNTRY FRY BATTER
Yields enough batter for 2 pounds of meat, fish, or poultry

1 egg, beaten
¼ cup milk
1 teaspoon poultry or fish seasoning
¼ teaspoon black pepper
1 teaspoon salt
¼ teaspoon baking soda
1 cup primary batter

Mix the egg and milk. Add the seasoning, black pepper, salt, and stir well. Add the baking soda and primary batter to the rest of the mixture and stir well. Cut up the meat and wash, clean, and drain it. Place each piece into the batter, covering all sides well. Place the meat in a hot frying pan with about ½ inch of oil. Cook each side until brown. Reduce the heat to low and continue to cook the meat for at least an additional 30 minutes, turning once. When done, drain and serve with mashed potatoes and gravy or sourdough biscuits and gravy.

PAPA'S NOOBLES
Yields 3 servings

Please note: There is no typo. It is "noobles." He calls them noobles. What can I say? Papa's a card. That's all.
1 cup primary batter
2 eggs, beaten, or 2 cups snow
¾ teaspoon baking soda

¾ teaspoon salt
2 tablespoons melted butter
2 to 3 cups white flour

Mix the ingredients well in a warm bowl. Add the flour ½ cup at a time, mixing well until the dough is elastic and will form a ball without sticking to the bowl. Put the dough on a flat, floured surface and divide into 2 pieces. Roll each half very thin; be sure to keep the dough floured well while rolling. Cut the dough into long strips about ½ inch wide and then cut the strips into 2 inch pieces. Flour noobles again and place on a flat pan or baking sheet. Cook the noobles in boiling chicken or beef broth until tender. This should take about 15 to 20 minutes.

PIZZA CRUST
Yields 1 pizza crust

1 cup primary batter
1 teaspoon sugar
1 teaspoon salt
2 teaspoons oil
1 cup flour (add more as needed)

Mix the ingredients in order, as listed. Add more flour if needed. Mix well until you have a thick, yet pliable, dough. Roll into a ball and let the dough proof for 30 minutes. Roll out your pizza dough, garnish it with all your favorite toppings or, in some cases, with whatever you have available. Bake at 350 degrees for 20 minutes or until it's done.

In regard to toppings, use whatever you like: mushrooms, sardines, rabbit, pineapple, oatmeal, squirrel, whatever. You can even forage for edible wild plants to top your pizza with. Make sure whatever you find is, indeed, edible, otherwise you may jeopardize your health. For reference, consult an edible plants guidebook.

DUMPLINGS

Yields 15 dumplings for stew

1 cup flour
1 teaspoon salt
1½ teaspoons baking soda
¼ cup shortening
1½ cups primary batter
¼ cup milk or cream

Mix the ingredients in order, stirring as little as possible until the dough is soft. Scoop up tablespoons of the dough and drop them onto the top of your stew. Try to get the dumplings to stay floating on top of the stew so they can rise. Cover the top quickly and don't open for 15 minutes or until the dumplings are done. Test for doneness by sticking them with a toothpick; if it comes out clean, they are cooked

For Thanksgiving 1991, we made a candlelight dinner of sourdough dumplings with government-issue dehydrated diced turkey with bannock and Kool-Aid. It wasn't Mom's but Dave seemed to like it anyway.

Chapter 6

Desserts

- Bite-size Peanut Butter Cookies   58
- Baker's Chocolate Cake   58
- Dazzlin' Dave's French Quarter Beignets   59
- Saturday Morning Cinnamon Rolls   60
- Robin Hood Oatmeal Pudding   61
- Mrs. Welburn's Oatmeal Raisin Cookies   62

THE WHOLE CONCEPT OF A DESSERT has increased pleasure while in the woods. Many factors come together to help transcend what would be a typical dessert in any domestic environment into a rapturous experience while in the woods. This comes from an earned hunger from physical exertion, gratification from the recipe's careful preparation, and, of course, having a sweet tooth. Most people have a sweet tooth, regardless of how successfully they disguise it. It is quite a natural tendency, and it is sheer bliss to feed one's appetite for sweets while sitting in a campfire's hypnotic glow. Have you ever met anyone who would naturally prefer ginseng root tea over chocolate milk, broccoli over strawberries, a guru-chew over candy bars, or puffed rice patties over freshly baked chocolate chip cookies? I didn't think so.

When in the backcountry few things instigate selfish behavior among campers like dessert time. "Are you going to eat that?" or "Can I lick the bowl?" or "That's all I get?" These questions come up a lot at campouts during dessert time. Whether they are spoken or unspoken is unimportant; the fact is, everyone's thinking it. Rightfully so. Not only is it natural to have an epicurean inclination towards sweets, but after hiking 15 miles or canoeing for 8 hours, it's a damn right! So exercise your right and try the following sourdough dessert recipes.

And don't feel guilty—sweet treats give you the energy you need in the backcountry.

The desserts I especially recommend are Dazzlin' Dave's French Quarter Beignets, Mrs. Welburn's Oatmeal Raisin Cookies, and Baker's Chocolate Cake. Each of these desserts has more than just flavor in its favor. Each recipe has a story to tell, and each has traveled a long distance to be here between the covers.

Dazzlin' Dave's recipe, created during our stay at the cabin, was a labor of love by my partner to create humanity's finest munchie food—the Dom Pérignon of pastries. Indeed, he did just that. I want to go on record and say that Dazzlin' Dave's French Quarter Beignets are the ultimate munchie food. Dave couldn't make enough of these. Each time he'd make them, we would eat them all in one day. He always tried to make more the next time so they would last, but the quantity would never suffice. We ate them in one day, too. Dave's beignets are so good that once we started eating them we really couldn't quit. I doubt you'll be able to stop either.

The second recipe came from the Welburn's of Churchill, Manitoba, the polar bear capital of the world. Mr. and Mrs. Welburn were kind enough to put us up in their cabin one night when we were stranded by a storm and sickness while on a canoe trip. Throughout the night my sweet tooth wouldn't let me get enough of Mrs. Welburn's oatmeal cookies. To help my insatiable hunger, she gave me the recipe.

My Baker's Chocolate Cake recipe is named as such because the only chocolate we had was Baker's brand, which is intended for baking and comes in bars with 1-ounce squares. Other companies sell the same type of chocolate bars for baking. We didn't let the lack of variety in chocolate spoil our enthusiasm for making chocolate cake. We used the Baker's chocolate with pride—and conservation since we only had a short supply on hand and no stores nearby to buy more.

Admittedly, sometimes we would eat our Baker's chocolate like candy, but we knew such behavior would cost us cake. Conversely, we knew making chocolate cake would cost us chocolate candy. Such is life with limited resources and no grocery store. Our gratification demanded sacrifice, and our taste buds demanded nothing less. Take heed, yours may too.

So you see, these are not just your typical recipes, they have a story all their own, a tale to tell, and flavorful delight to share.

Enjoy!

BITE-SIZE PEANUT BUTTER COOKIES

Yields 4 dozen cookies

½ cup soft butter
1 cup brown sugar
½ cup peanut butter
1 egg, beaten
1 cup primary batter
½ teaspoon salt
½ teaspoon baking soda
¾ cup white flour

Mix the ingredients in order, as listed. Drop the batter by the spoonful onto a greased baking sheet. Bake at 375 degrees for 12 to 15 minutes or until golden brown. Cool on a wire rack if possible.

BAKER'S CHOCOLATE CAKE

Yields 1 2-layer-thick chocolate cake

½ cup cocoa or 2¼ squares Baker's chocolate
1 teaspoon baking soda
1 cup boiling water
½ cup butter
½ cup shortening
2 cups sugar
3 eggs, beaten
1 teaspoon vanilla
1 teaspoon salt
½ cup milk
1½ cups primary batter
1 cup flour

Mix the first 3 ingredients together and let sit for 20 minutes. Then add the eggs, vanilla, and salt. Beat mixture together. Then add the milk, primary batter, and flour, mixing well. Pour the batter into a Jell-O® mold or cake pan and bake at 350 degrees for 30 minutes or until done. Remove from the pan and let cool on wire racks if possible.

DAZZLIN' DAVE'S FRENCH QUARTER BEIGNETS

Yields about 20 beignets

1½ cups primary batter
1 egg, beaten
¼ teaspoons vanilla
¼ cup milk
2 tablespoons cooking oil
2 cups flour
¼ teaspoon baking soda
¼ cup sugar
¾ teaspoon salt

Mix the ingredients in a large bowl, adding the flour ½ cup at a time. Mix well. Place dough onto a flat floured surface and knead until dough firms up, but is soft and easy to manage. Roll out the dough to ½-inch thickness. Using

Here is Dave making his famous beignets. I could never match his skill at making them. He was the master.

a cookie cutter or whatever will work (I used a metal ring from a roll of bandaging tape in the medical kit), cut beignets into circles about 2 inches in diameter. Gather scraps into a ball and roll out and cut again until all dough is used up. Place them on a lightly floured or greased flat surface and set in a warm place for 30 minutes to proof. Meanwhile, in a large bowl mix:

> 2 cups confectioner's (powdered) sugar
> 1 cup brown sugar
> ¼ cup cinnamon

This is your powder coating for the beignets. As the dough continues to proof, prepare a skillet or Dutch oven with cooking oil and heat it until it's super hot. When the beignets are done proofing, place a couple at a time in the grease to fry. Fry on both sides until they are brown and puffed up like a doughnut without a hole. When done, remove the beignets from the grease and place in the cinnamon and sugar mixture and roll them around in the powder to coat them. Repeat this process until all are coated with powder sugar. The beignets are best served with coffee while warm. Feel free to experiment by adding raisins or cinnamon to the dough for variation.

SATURDAY MORNING CINNAMON ROLLS
Yields 14 rolls

> 1½ cups primary batter
> ¼ teaspoon vanilla
> ¾ cup milk
> ¼ cup sugar
> 1 tablespoon cinnamon
> 1 tablespoon melted butter
> 1 teaspoon salt
> 2 cups flour

Mix the ingredients, adding the flour ½ cup at a time. Knead the dough on a flat floured surface until smooth and soft. Place the dough in a large container for 2 hours to proof, or until double in bulk. Turn dough out onto a floured board and roll to ½-inch thickness.

Brush dough with additional butter and sprinkle liberally with an additional ¼ cup of sugar and 1 teaspoon cinnamon mixed together. Roll dough into a cylinder. Brush with melted butter and sprinkle again with sugar and cinnamon mixture, then cut the cylinder into equal sections or rolls. Place the rolls on a greased baking sheet, cover, and let sit in a warm place for 30 minutes to proof. Remove cover and bake rolls at 325 degrees for 25 to 30 minutes or until done. If possible, let them cool on a wire rack. Cover with butter and honey and serve warm.

ROBIN HOOD OATMEAL PUDDING
Yields 5 servings

1 cup primary batter
¾ cup sugar
¾ teaspoon salt
1 teaspoon baking soda
1 teaspoon cinnamon
1 cup quick-cooking oats
¾ cup chopped dates
3 tablespoons butter
1½ teaspoons vanilla
½ cup honey

Put all ingredients except the honey in a large bowl. Mix well. Grease a 1-quart bowl or 1-pound coffee can and pour the batter inside. Cover the bowl tightly with wax paper or aluminum foil. Place the pudding bowl inside a pan of boiling water, but be sure to elevate the pudding off the bottom of the pan in some manner. A rack will work, or putting stones on the bottom works well. The water in the pan should reach halfway up the pudding container. Cover the pan of boiling water and let the pudding steam for 90 minutes. When done, remove pudding from the bowl and put on a serving plate. Cover with honey and serve.

MRS. WELBURN'S OATMEAL RAISIN COOKIES

Yields 3 dozen cookies, depending on the size

1½ cups primary batter
1 cup shortening
1 cup white sugar
¼ cup brown sugar
1 egg or 1 cup snow
¼ cup milk
1 teaspoon salt
1 teaspoon cinnamon
3 cups oat (quick-cooking or rolled)
1 cup raisins

Mix the ingredients in order, as listed, stirring after each addition. Drop the batter by the spoonful onto a greased baking sheet. Bake at 400 degrees for 12 to 15 minutes or until done.

Chapter 7

Pancakes & Waffles

- Bacon Pancakes   65
- Apple Pancakes   66
- Chocolate Waffles   66
- Cornmeal Pancakes   67
- Cornmeal Waffles   67
- Oat Pancakes   68
- Rice Pancakes   68
- Russian Pancakes   69
- Sourdough Waffles   69
- Traditional Sourdough Pancakes   70
- Whole Wheat Pancakes   70
- Whole Wheat Waffles   71

TO ENSURE THE FLAVOR and overall success of your recipe, it's important to keep some things in mind. For instance, the cooking technique for a pancake is different than the cooking technique for a waffle.

To cook a pancake, take a spoonful of pancake batter and place it on a hot, lightly greased skillet. Space the pancakes so that they do not touch, and fry them until air bubbles begin to appear on the top side. When this happens, slide a spatula under the edge of each pancake and lift it just enough to look underneath and see if the bottom is browned and done frying. If it is, flip the pancake and fry the other side until it's browned as well. The most important thing when frying pancakes is to be patient and wait until it is done frying before you try to flip it. Otherwise, you'll end up with a gooey mess inside your skillet and your fellow campers may lose their appetites.

Preparing waffles is a different process and may be easier for you than cooking pancakes. The main difference is the waffle iron in which they are cooked. These can be purchased at your local camping outfitter, sporting goods store, or stores such as K-Mart or Wal-Mart. Simply place ¼ to ½ cup of the batter at a time inside a preheated waffle iron and cook until steam appears. Do not overfill the waffle iron, or the batter will run out the sides as it rises. Precious batter will be lost, and you will have a mess to clean up. Open the waffle iron to check for doneness. If the waffles don't stick and are golden brown, they are done. Flip them out and serve.

Pancakes were a big part of my wilderness diet. Really, when it came down to it, my options for breakfast were as limitless as my imagination. When I was hungry, and the need to be fed was greater than my want of a gourmet meal, I would whip up some oatmeal with tea or coffee. Otherwise, pancakes were prepared a couple of times a week, if not more.

It's quite a process to fix pancakes—I'd be a liar if I said it was a skill of instinct. In reality, the development of my ability to fix killer pancakes was a direct result of the sacrificed lives of innocent pancakes, born prematurely to die by the heat of the skillet. Sourdough pancakes were a favorite to eat. They were the most filling and best tasting. In addition to all of that, the leftovers made great snacks or target practice, whichever you prefer. While living in the cabin, sourdough pancakes were also a favorite amongst neighboring squirrels, weasels, and Canada jays.

I'll never forget the time that I was awakened by a small pine squirrel that had managed to get himself into the loft where I was sleeping. The noise as he scurried across the floor disturbed me enough for me to open my eyes. He had entered the cabin through a small gap between a ceiling log and a wall log. He often would come in early in the morning and search for scraps lying around. If scraps weren't available, he would try to open a box or bag of goodies himself. This morning, however, he had managed to find one sourdough pancake left over from the day before. Upon discovering that the pancake smelled better than pinecone seeds, the pine squirrel secured the pancake between his jaws, and was en route to his nest with it when I noticed him.

First of all, I was in awe of the animal's ability to gracefully maneuver the pancake. I likened it to the way one would handle a priceless piece of art. To the squirrel, no doubt, the pancake was a priceless find, worthy of all the effort to keep it safe.

The squirrel was trying to take the pancake through the gap from which he had entered, but since the pancake was wider than the hole, he ran into a problem. When pushing with the pancake still in his mouth, the squirrel couldn't get it to fit through. Frustrated and perplexed, the little creature put down the goodie and began to stare at the gap and the pancake. How was he going to get this precious treasure through the hole?

Having determined a strategy, he bounded over the pancake and dashed into the gap, out of my sight. A second later, the squirrel stuck his head back through the gap, grabbed the pancake between his jaws and pulled it through the hole. Success!

Fortunately, we humans don't have to go through all of that for the mouth-watering, delicious flavor of sourdough pancakes. All we have to do is follow the recipe, fry them until golden brown, and hope they fit in our mouths.

BACON PANCAKES
Yields 4 3-inch pancakes

1½ cups primary batter
1 cup flour
2 eggs or 2 cups snow
3 tablespoons sugar
2 tablespoons melted butter
1 teaspoon salt
½ cup milk
6 to 8 fried bacon slices crumbled

Mix the ingredients in order, as listed. Let the batter rest for 10 minutes. Spoon the batter for each pancake onto a preheated, lightly greased skillet. Fry until the bottom is browned, then flip. Once both sides are browned, serve hot with toppings of your choice. *Hint:* For an even stronger bacon taste, crumble a little bacon into the pancake syrup or other topping.

APPLE PANCAKES
Yields 8 2-inch pancakes

1½ cups primary batter
1 cup flour
2 eggs or 2 cups snow
3 tablespoons sugar
2 tablespoons melted butter
1 teaspoon salt
½ cup milk
1 cup sliced apples
1 teaspoon nutmeg
1 teaspoon vanilla

Mix the ingredients in order, as listed. Let the batter rest for 10 minutes. Spoon the batter for each pancake onto a preheated, lightly greased skillet. Fry until the top glazes over and the surface no longer appears shiny, then flip. The bottom should be a perfect golden brown. Once both sides are browned, serve hot with peanut butter and honey.

CHOCOLATE WAFFLES
Yields 3 6-inch square waffles

1½ cups primary batter
2 eggs
3 tablespoons sugar
½ teaspoon salt
½ cup cocoa
½ teaspoon vanilla
½ cup butter
1 cup milk

Mix the ingredients in order, as listed. Pour the batter for each waffle onto a preheated waffle iron. Cook each waffle until the steam disappears. If waffles are golden brown, they're done. Serve hot with toppings such as whipped cream and chocolate syrup and dig in.

CORNMEAL PANCAKES

Yields 10 2-inch pancakes

1½ cups primary batter
2 eggs or 2 cups snow
3 tablespoons sugar
2 tablespoons melted butter
1 teaspoon salt
1 cup milk
1 cup yellow cornmeal

Mix the ingredients in order, as listed. Let batter sit for 10 minutes. Spoon the batter for each pancake onto a preheated, lightly greased skillet. Fry until the bottom is browned, then flip. Once both sides are browned, serve hot with your favorite toppings.

CORNMEAL WAFFLES

Yields 3 6-inch square waffles

1½ cups primary batter
½ cup milk
3 eggs
3 teaspoons sugar
½ teaspoon salt
¼ cup butter
1 cup cornmeal

Mix the ingredients in order, as listed. Pour batter onto a preheated waffle iron. Cook waffles in the iron until the steam disappears. If the waffles are golden brown, they're done. Serve hot with toppings such as honey, maple syrup, or jam.

OAT PANCAKES

Yields 15 2-inch pancakes

1½ cups primary batter
2 eggs or 2 cups snow
3 tablespoons sugar
2 tablespoons melted butter or margarine
1½ teaspoons salt
1 cup milk
1 cup oats

Mix the ingredients in order, as listed. Let the batter rest for 10 minutes. Spoon the batter for each pancake onto a preheated, lightly greased skillet. Fry until the bottom is browned, then flip. Once both sides are browned, serve hot with toppings of your choice. Maple syrup is my favorite for this dish. Wild berries are always a great addition, but you must be absolutely sure the ones you use are edible. Consult an edible plants guidebook before indulging in unfamiliar wild berries or plants of any kind.

RICE PANCAKES

Yields 4 3-inch pancakes

1½ cups primary batter
1 cup flour
2 eggs or 2 cups snow
3 tablespoons sugar
2 tablespoons melted butter
1 teaspoon salt
½ cup milk
½ cup cooked rice
½ teaspoon vanilla

Mix the ingredients. Let batter sit for 10 minutes. Spoon the batter for each pancake onto a preheated, lightly greased skillet. Fry until the bottom is browned, then flip. Once both sides are browned, serve hot with butter and honey.

RUSSIAN PANCAKES
Yields 15 Russian pancakes

1 cup primary batter
1 tablespoon sugar
¼ cup milk
2 eggs, beaten or 2 cups snow
1 teaspoon baking soda
½ teaspoon salt
½ cup flour
2 tablespoons Butter

Mix the ingredients in order, as listed. Let the batter stand for 10 minutes. Melt 2 tablespoons butter in a skillet and put about 2 teaspoons of batter in the skillet to make pancakes about the size of a silver dollar.

SOURDOUGH WAFFLES
Yields 3 6-inch square waffles

1½ cups primary batter
2 eggs
3 teaspoons sugar
½ teaspoon salt
¼ cup melted butter
¼ cup milk

Mix the ingredients in order, as listed. Pour the batter for each waffle into a preheated waffle iron. Cook the waffles in the iron until the steam disappears. If the waffles are golden brown, they're done. Serve hot with toppings such as honey, maple syrup, or jam.

TRADITIONAL SOURDOUGH PANCAKES

Yields 5 large pancakes

1½ cups primary batter
½ cup white flour
1 egg or 1 cup snow
1 tablespoon sugar
1 tablespoon melted butter
¾ teaspoon salt
2 tablespoons milk

Mix the ingredients in order, as listed. Let the batter rest for 10 minutes. Spoon the batter for each pancake onto a preheated, lightly greased skillet. Fry until the bottom is browned, then flip. Once both sides are browned, serve hot with toppings of your choice. Butter and honey are my favorites.

WHOLE WHEAT PANCAKES

Yields 5 large pancakes

1½ cups primary batter
2 eggs or 2 cups snow
2 tablespoons sugar
2 tablespoons melted butter
1 teaspoon salt
½ cup milk
1 cup whole wheat flour

Mix the ingredients in order, as listed. Let the batter sit for 10 minutes. Spoon the batter for each pancake onto a preheated, lightly greased skillet. Fry until the bottom is browned, then flip. Once both sides are browned, serve hot with toppings of your choice. Butter and honey are my favorites.

WHOLE WHEAT WAFFLES
Yields 3 6-inch square waffles

1½ cups primary batter
½ cup milk
2 eggs separated
3 teaspoons sugar
½ teaspoon salt
¼ cup melted butter
½ cup whole wheat flour

Mix the ingredients in order, as listed. Pour the batter for each waffle onto a preheated waffle iron. Cook the waffles in the iron until the steam disappears. If waffles are golden brown, stick a fork in them because they're done. Serve hot with your best toppings.

Top 10
Miscellaneous Uses
of Sourdough

BESIDES DELICIOUS PANCAKES, breads, desserts and entrees, sourdough leads other lives. It is an epicurean double agent, posing as a simple leavener, when in fact it is a complex organism that serves many roles. The top ten miscellaneous uses of sourdough are:

10. Beer. It is possible to make sourdough beer that will get you drunk if you can stand the taste. The recipe is this: Mix 3 cups of rice, edible berries, or barley (any edible fruit or grain will do) with 4 cups of sugar, 3 cups of primary batter, and 2 gallons of warm water. Let this mixture sit for 5 days in a warm, dry place to ferment. Then bottoms up!

9. Glue. Sourdough, once allowed to dry, will harden like cement. This makes it a great bonding agent. At the cabin, sourdough was used many times to repair broken wooden objects such as the spatula and chairs.

8. Gift. Sourdough makes a great gift. It represents the gift of food, which ensures health and sustains life—and that's the best kind of gift there is. Our sourdough crock and starter were given to Dave and me before we went to the cabin. It fed us and sustained us and gave us much pleasure.

7. Tester for stain removers. If you ever are considering buying a stain remover like those you see for carpets, clothing, etc., and are having a hard time deciding which one to get, try this: Take some sourdough starter and smear it all over the sales clerk's jacket. (Be sure to ask permission.) Let it dry until hardened. Then use the stain remover in question to try and remove the sourdough stain. Whichever one works, buy it. However, what you may find is that the stain cannot be removed. It's quite possible none of the cleaning solutions will work and you will have to buy the clerk a new jacket. In my experience, once sourdough has a chance to dry it is impossible to remove. So let this be a lesson!

6. **Incense.** Sourdough is quite aromatic. It will fill the room with its beer-like aroma.

5. **Mouse trap.** If you are having problems with mice invading your camp and forgot to bring traps, just place little piles of sourdough starter strategically so that the mice will find it, wander into it, and get stuck.

4. **Family heirloom.** Back during the sourdough craze, and in the wilderness where food was sometimes scarce, it was very normal for families to pass crocks of sourdough starter from generation to generation. It was the most valued and precious possession in the household.

3. **Caulk.** Sourdough is great to fill those little holes around the cabin window the winds of winter seem to love.

2. **Weapon.** See #1.

1. **Food fights.** Self-explanatory.

You see, there is more to sourdough than meets the eye—or the mouth. It is the chameleon of cookery, the *tour de flavor*, the wind in your sails, the spring in your step, the hip in your hop, your sunshine your only sunshine, your happiness when skies are gray, the candle under your bushel, the pickle in your pocket, and your nutritional safety belt and helmet from hunger. So use it. You will be glad you did.

Epilogue

MUCH TIME HAS PASSED since I began writing this book by candlelight at the cabin, yet it seems like just moments ago. I think back to those days and know they were special beyond words. I often try to explain to people some of those events that Dave Scott and I saw (Aurora Borealis), heard (silence), felt (60 degrees below zero), tasted (sourdough pancakes), and smelled (spring), but, it's difficult. One must use words very effectively to convey the sensation of the experience.

Unfortunately, you were not there with me and Dave at the cabin, counting dozens of bug bites on a July afternoon, watching the boiling spectrum of Northern Lights that filled the night sky, suffering from frostbite at 60-below zero. Therefore, it is impossible for you to know what it was *really* like. Dave and I will often phone each other to reminisce, saying, "Remember when . . . ." So, this is why we must try to use words to remember, record and share the adventure, mystery, and romance of our wilderness refuge.

Within these pages, I tried to help you learn something you can use and enjoy. I hope I succeeded. But, if there were a person whose words can transport you to that little rustic cabin I love so much, it would be my partner, Dave Scott. With a delicate touch and precision Dave has written *Paradise Creek,* soon to be published by AlpenBooks Press. That book is not just another journal of some distant adventure, but a heartfelt look at two young men on their rite of passage from the status quo of civilization into the beautiful, yet dangerous, wilderness of northern Canada.

Read it while you eat some sourdough bread.

Scott Power
June 2004

Appendices

A. Trail Stove Tips

Selection

The most practical trail stoves for cooking in the outdoors are not necessarily those that burn the hottest, or are the most expensive. Use these guidelines as a basis for stove selection:

Stability: Stove stability is important. Avoid stoves that threaten to topple. Look for a low-to-the-ground profile.

Ease-of-starting: Some stoves come equipped with pumps for easier starting and more efficient use in cold weather. Stay away from stoves that require considerable pumping to start or maintain a flame.

Wind susceptibility: The first time you have to build a rock wall around your stove to keep it perking in the wind, you'll understand the importance of a good windscreen. Avoid aluminum foil windscreens that interfere with the use of skillet handles.

Fuel and heat output: White gasoline, propane, butane, kerosene, or multifuel? For winter cooking you need blowtorch performance. A winter stove should boil a quart of water at sea level in an uncovered pot in less than five minutes.

If you want efficiency, stick with stoves that burn *white gas* or *propane* if you can carry the heavy fuel tanks.

The efficiency of *butane* is directly proportional to heat and altitude. In below freezing weather, butane stoves don't work at all. On mountain tops, because of the low air pressure, they work fine. The typical butane stove requires at least eight minutes to boil a quart of water at 70-degrees Fahrenheit, at sea level.

Kerosene stoves burn hot and are very safe (they can't explode). However, kerosene is oily and smelly—the reason why it's unpopular. But, if you're traveling in Europe, where white gas is unavailable, kerosene is the logical choice.

Multifuel stoves don't burn as hot as equivalent gas models and they are much more expensive. Get a multifuel stove only if you need it.

Simmering heat: High heat output is great, but so is a low-simmering flame. Some of the best winter stoves (like the MSR X-GK) are not adjustable enough for gourmet cooking.

Weight: Some of the most reliable and versatile trail stoves are relatively heavy by backpacking standards. Examples include the Optimus 111B and 111 Hiker, the Phoenix Mountaineer, and the venerable Coleman twin burner.

Ruggedness: If a part looks weak, it probably is. If there's a plastic knob, which can burn or break, it will. If there are components that may be lost, count on it. The best trail stoves are rugged, compact, and have no parts to break, burn, assemble, or lose.

Maintenance

Fuel: For greatest efficiency and trouble free operation, use Coleman fuel in your gasoline stove. MSR markets its own super-refined white gas that is highly regarded, but expensive. These pre-filtered fuels burn clean and have extremely high heat output.

Filling: Don't fill gasoline stoves more than ¾ full. You need air space to generate pressure.

Emptying: Empty the fuel from your stove after each trip, and burn dry what you can't pour out. Fuel left in stoves leaves varnishes, which clog jets and filters—the major reason for stove failure.

Storing: Keep your stove in a fabric sack when it's not in use. This will prevent dust and debris from getting into the working parts.

Lubrication: Lubricate leather pump washers with high-temperature gun oil. Avoid use of multipurpose and vegetable oils, which may break down and gum up valves.

B. Useful Common Weights and Measures and Food Equivalents

3 teaspoons = 1 tablespoon

2 tablespoons = 1 liquid ounce

16 tablespoon = 1 cup

1 cup = 8 ounces

2 cups = 1 pint

4 cups = 1 quart

½ lb. margarine = 1 cup

1 lb. granulated sugar = 2¼ cups

1 lb. brown sugar = 2¼ to 2½ cups, packed

1 lb. confectioners' (powdered) sugar = 3½ cups

1 ounce butter or margarine = 2 tablespoons fat

¼ lb. or 1 stick butter or margarine = ½ cup fat

1 lb. butter or margarine = 2 cups fat

1 cup milk and 1 tablespoon vinegar = 1 cup sour milk

⅓ cup butter, ⅔ cup milk, and
1 tablespoon vinegar = 1 cup sour cream

1 square baking chocolate = 1 ounce

1 square baking chocolate = 3½ tablespoons dry cocoa and
1 tablespoon butter

½ cup cocoa and 2¼ tablespoons butter = 2¼ squares baking chocolate

13 egg yolks = 1 cup yolks

9 egg whites = 1 cup whites

1 cup snow = 1 egg

1 lb. all-purpose flour, sifted = 4 cups

1 lb. cake flour, sifted = 4½ cups

1 lb. cornmeal = 3 cups

1 lb. rice = 2⅓ cups uncooked rice

1 cup chopped nuts = about ¼ lb

64 marshmallows = 1 lb

1 medium onion = 2 tablespoons minced dry onions

1 tablespoon fresh herbs = ½ teaspoons dried herbs, or
¼ teaspoon dried, powdered herbs

No. 10 can holds about 12 cups of water

1 level, full Sierra cup holds a little more than 1 cup liquid

1 standard-sized plastic insulated cup holds about 1⅓ cup liquid

Bibliography

Forgey, William W., M.D. *Wilderness Medicine, Beyond First Aid*, 5th Edition. Guilford, CT: Globe Pequot Press, 1999.

Jacobson, Cliff. *Basic Essentials Cooking in the Outdoors*, 2nd Edition. Guilford, CT: Globe Pequot Press, 1999.

Jacobson, Cliff. *Camping's Top Secrets: A Lexicon of Camping Tips Only the Experts Know*, 2nd Edition. Guilford, CT: Globe Pequot Press, 1998.

Kephart, Horace. *Camp Cookery*, Creative Cookbooks, 2001.

———. *Camping and Woodcraft: A Handbook for Vacation Campers and for Travelers in the Wilderness*. Knoxville, TN: University of Tennessee Press, 1988.

Rutstrum, Calvin. *The New Way of the Wilderness: The Classic Guide to Survival in the Wild*. Minneapolis, MN, reprint edition: University of Minnesota Press, 2000.

Index

bannock 21–22, 42

batters 33–34, 53

beignets 59–60

biscuits 42

bread 44, 46–47, 49, 51

bread sticks 37

cake 48, 58

campfire

   baking on 20–23

containers 31–32

cookies 58, 62

cornbread 45

crackers 39, 40

double-pan oven 23–24

dumplings 55

Dutch oven 22–23, 26

egg substitute 31

fats 31

flour 28–29

French bread 49–51

ingredients 27–31

Jell-O mold oven 24–25

leaveners 29–30

miscellaneous uses 72–73

muffins 45, 48

noobles 53–54

noodles *(see noobles)*

pancakes 63–70

pizza crust 54

pretzels 39

primary batter 33–34

pudding 61

reflector oven 20–21

rolls 44, 60–61

scones 40

skillet oven 21–22

special instructions 32

starters 33–34

stovetop camp oven 26

sweeteners 30–31

trail stove

   baking on 23–25

   tips 75–76

waffles 63–64, 66, 67, 69, 71

weights and measures 77

wood stove

   baking on 25–26

ABOUT THE AUTHOR:

IN 1991 SCOTT POWER lived in a wilderness log cabin near the Arctic Circle, 120 miles from the nearest grocery store. Scott quickly learned to use sourdough starter to make his own bread and pancakes. He has written this cookbook to share his sourdough tricks, tips, and recipes—along with some tales of his adventure in the beautiful wilderness of northern Canada. Scott currently resides in Santa Monica, California.